AMAZING ANIMALS OF THE WORLD 3

Volume 2

Butterfly, Indian Leaf — Dormouse, Garden

GROLIER

an imprint of

SCHOLASTIC

Scholastic Library Publishing

www.scholastic.com/librarypublishing

First published 2006 by Grolier, an imprint of Scholastic Library Publishing

© 2006 Scholastic Library Publishing

For information address the publisher: Grolier, Scholastic Library Publishing
90 Old Sherman Turnpike
Danbury, CT 06816

10 digit: Set ISBN: 0-7172-6179-4; Volume ISBN: 0-7172-6181-6
13 digit: Set ISBN: 978-0-7172-6179-6; Volume ISBN: 978-0-7172-6181-9

Printed and bound in the U.S.A.

Library of Congress Cataloging-in-Publications Data:
Amazing animals of the world 3.
p.cm.
Includes indexes.
Contents: v. 1. Abalone, Black–Butterfly, Giant Swallowtail -- v. 2. Butterfly, Indian Leaf–Dormouse, Garden -- v. 3. Duck, Ferruginous–Glassfish, Indian -- v. 4. Glider, Sugar–Isopod, Freshwater -- v. 5. Jackal, Side-Striped–Margay -- v. 6. Markhor–Peccary, Collared -- v. 7. Pelican, Brown–Salamander, Spotted -- v. 8. Salamander, Two Lined–Spider, Barrel -- v. 9. Spider, Common House–Tuna, Albacore -- v. 10. Tunicate, Light-Bulb–Zebra, Grevy's.
ISBN 0-7172–6179–4 (set : alk. paper) -- ISBN 0–7172–6180–8 (v. 1 : alk. paper) -- ISBN 0-7172-6181–6 (v. 2 : alk. paper) -- ISBN 0-7172-6182–4 (v. 3 : alk. paper) -- ISBN 0-7172-6183–2 (v. 4 : alk. paper) -- ISBN 0-7172-6184–0 (v. 5 : alk. paper) -- ISBN 0-7172-6185–9 (v. 6 : alk. paper) -- ISBN 0-7172-6186–7 (v. 7 : alk. paper) -- ISBN 0-7172-6187–5 (v. 8 : alk. paper) -- ISBN 0-7172-6188–3 (v. 9 : alk. paper) -- ISBN 0-7172-6189–1 (v. 10 : alk.paper)
1. Animals--Juvenile literature. I. Grolier (Firm) II. Title: Amazing animals of the world three.
QL49.A455 2006
590—dc22
2006010870

About This Set

Amazing Animals of the World 3 brings you pictures of 400 exciting creatures, and important information about how and where they live.

Each page shows just one species, or individual type, of animal. They all fall into seven main categories, or groups, of animals (classes and phylums scientifically) identified on each page with an icon (picture)—amphibians, arthropods, birds, fish, mammals, other invertebrates, and reptiles. Short explanations of what these group names mean, and other terms used commonly in the set, appear on page 4 in the Glossary.

Scientists use all kinds of groupings to help them sort out the types of animals that exist today and once wandered the earth (extinct species). *Kingdoms*, *classes*, *phylums*, *genus*, and *species* are among the key words here that are also explained in the Glossary.

Where animals live is important to know as well. Each of the species in this set lives in a particular place in the world, which you can see outlined on the map on each page. And in those places, the animals tend to favor a particular habitat—an environment the animal finds suitable for life—with food, shelter, and safety from predators that might eat it. There they also find ways to coexist with other animals in the area that might eat somewhat different food, use different homes, and so on.

Each of the main habitats is named on the page and given an icon, or picture, to help you envision it. The habitat names are further defined in the Glossary on page 4.

As well as being part of groups like species, animals fall into other categories that help us understand their lives or behavior. You will find these categories in the Glossary on page 4, where you will learn about carnivores, herbivores, and other types of animals.

And there is more information you might want about an animal—its size, diet, where it lives, and how it carries on its species—the way it creates its young. All these facts and more appear in the data boxes at the top of each page.

Finally, the set is arranged alphabetically by the most common name of the species. That puts most beetles, for example, together in a group so you can compare them easily.

But some animals' names are not so common, and they don't appear near others like them. For instance, the chamois is a kind of goat or antelope. To find animals that are similar—or to locate any species—look in the Index at the end of each book in the set (pages 45–48). It lists all animals by their various names (you will find the Giant South American River Turtle under Turtle, Giant South American River, and also under its other name— Arrau). And you will find all birds, fish, and so on gathered under their broader groupings.

Similarly, smaller like groups appear in the Set Index as well—butterflies include swallowtails and blues, for example.

Table of Contents
Volume 2

Glossary

Amphibians—species usually born from eggs in water or wet places, which change (metamorphose) into land animals. Frogs and salamanders are typical. They breathe through their skin mainly and have no scales.

Arctic and Antarctic—icy, cold, dry areas at the ends of the globe that lack trees but see small plants grown in thawed areas (tundra). Penguins and seals are common inhabitants.

Arthropods—animals with segmented bodies, hard outer skin, and jointed legs, such as spiders and crabs.

Birds—born from eggs, these creatures have wings and often can fly. Eagles, pigeons, and penguins are all birds, though penguins cannot fly through the air.

Carnivores—they are animals that eat other animals. Many species do eat each other sometimes, and a few eat dead animals. Lions kill their prey and eat it, while vultures clean up dead bodies of animals.

Cities, Towns, and Farms—places where people live and have built or used the land and share it with many species. Sometimes these animals live in human homes or just nearby.

Class—part or division of a phylum.

Deserts—dry, often warm areas where animals often are more active on cooler nights or near water sources. Owls, scorpions, and jack rabbits are common in American deserts.

Endangered—some animals in this set are marked as endangered because it is possible they will become extinct soon.

Extinct—these species have died out altogether for whatever reason.

Family—part of an order.

Fish—water animals (aquatic) that typically are born from eggs and breathe through gills. Trout and eels are fish, though whales and dolphins are not (they are mammals).

Forests and Mountains—places where evergreen (coniferous) and leaf-shedding (deciduous) trees are common, or that rise in elevation to make cool, separate habitats. Rain forests are different. (see Rain forests)

Fresh Water—lakes, rivers, and the like carry fresh water (unlike Oceans and Shores, where the water is salty). Fish and birds abound, as do insects, frogs, and mammals.

Genus—part of a family.

Grasslands—habitats with few trees and light rainfall. Grasslands often lie between forests and deserts, and they are home to birds, coyotes, antelope, and snakes, as well as many other kinds of animals.

Herbivores—these animals eat mainly plants. Typically they are hoofed animals (ungulates) that are common on grasslands, such as antelope or deer. Domestic (nonwild) ones are cows and horses.

Hibernators—species that live in harsh areas with very cold winters slow down their functions then and sort of sleep through the hard times.

Invertebrates—animals that lack backbones or internal skeletons. Many, such as insects and shrimp, have hard outer coverings. Clams and worms are also invertebrates.

Kingdom—the largest division of species. Commonly there are understood to be five kingdoms: animals, plants, fungi, protists, and monerans.

Mammals—these creatures usually bear live young and feed them on milk from the mother. A few lay eggs (monotremes like the platypus) or nurse young in a pouch (marsupials like opossums and kangaroos).

Migrators—some species spend different seasons in different places, moving to where more food, warmth, or safety can be found. Birds often do this, sometimes over long distances, but other types of animals also move seasonally, including fish and mammals.

Oceans and Shores—seawater is salty, often deep, and huge. In it live many fish, invertebrates, and even some mammals, such as whales. On the shore, birds and other creatures often gather.

Order—part of a class.

Phylum—part of a kingdom.

Rain forests—here huge trees grow among many other plants helped by the warm, wet environment. Thousands of species of animals also live in these rich habitats.

Reptiles—these species have scales, lungs to breathe, and lay eggs or give birth to live young. Dinosaurs are thought to have been reptiles, while today the class includes turtles, snakes, lizards, and crocodiles.

Scientific name—the genus and species name of a creature in Latin. For instance, Canis lupus is the wolf. Scientific names avoid the confusion possible with common names in any one language or across languages.

Species—a group of the same type of living thing. Part of an order.

Subspecies—a variant but quite similar part of a species.

Territorial—many animals mark out and defend a patch of ground as their home area. Birds and mammals may call quite small or quite large spots their territories.

Vertebrates—animals with backbones and skeletons under their skins

Indian Leaf Butterfly
Kallima paralekta

Length of the Body: about 2 inches
Wingspan: 4 to 4¾ inches
Diet: leaves (caterpillar); fruit nectar (adult)

Method of Reproduction: egg layer
Home: Asia
Order: Butterflies and moths
Family: Four-footed butterflies

 Forests and Mountains

Arthropods

© E. R. DEGGINGER / COLOR PIC, INC.

In the world of insects, some species have evolved brilliant colors and markings for attracting mates or warning predators. Other species are drab and blend with their surroundings, making it difficult for predators to spot them. The Indian leaf butterfly has both qualities. The top sides of its wings are a rich purplish blue, with a bright orange band of color across the front. But the undersides of the butterfly's wings are the dull colors of a dry, dead leaf.

When flying or resting with its wings open, the Indian leaf butterfly is a bright, eye-popping jewel. But when disturbed, it darts away and settles again with its wings closed. In this position, only the camouflaged underside of its wings can be seen. Different individuals mimic different stages of a dying leaf. Some are greenish under the wings, like a leaf that is not entirely dead, while others are gray or brownish red.

The leaf butterfly's expert mimicry does not stop with its coloration. The creature perches with its wings folded over its back at the exact same angle that leaves grow from a stem. In addition, the tips of this butterfly's hind wings have special points that resemble leafstalks. And just as insects chew tiny holes in real leaves, the butterfly has tiny clear areas on its wings through which light can be seen.

Lesser Purple Emperor Butterfly
Apatura ilia

Wingspan: 2½ to 3 inches
Diet: willow and poplar leaves (caterpillar)
Method of Reproduction: egg layer

Home: Europe and Asia
Order: Butterflies and moths
Family: Brush-footed butterflies

 Forests and Mountains

 Arthropods

© LEROY SIMON / VISUALS UNLIMITED

The colorful lesser purple emperor butterfly is a powerful flier with a muscular body and a large head. It is most abundant in lightly wooded forests, where it darts in and out of sunny, open areas. Male emperors often battle over territories, with the stronger male chasing a weaker one far from his turf. Sometimes, by the time the victor returns home, another male has stolen his domain.

The male purple emperor also chases any female that flies into his territory. But the purpose of this chase is to breed. Purple emperors often mate high in the trees. The female usually chooses a lower spot to deposit her small, gumdrop-shaped eggs.

The purple emperor's caterpillar is even more colorful than its attractive butterfly parents. Reaching a length of up to 2 inches, the slender green caterpillar is decorated with yellow-and-white spots and diagonal stripes. The belly and head are blue, and the pale green horns are tipped in red. The caterpillar feeds on willow and poplar leaves until midsummer, when it dangles from a leaf and spins a cocoon around its body. Inside, the caterpillar transforms into an adult butterfly, emerging in late summer. These late-summer emperors mate and lay eggs in September. The caterpillars that hatch in autumn sew themselves beneath small silk pads on leaves, twigs, and flower buds and emerge as butterflies the following spring.

Ringlet (Meadow Brown) Butterfly
Maniola jurtina

Wingspan: 1½ to 2 inches
Diet: grasses
Method of Reproduction: egg layer

Home: Europe
Order: Butterflies and moths
Family: Satyrs and wood nymphs

 Grasslands

 Arthropods

© ROBERT PICKETT / CORBIS

The ringlet, or meadow brown, is a butterfly noted for the distinctive eyespot on each front wing. This spot is usually black or brown with a distinct white "bull's-eye." Many male ringlets lack this spot within a spot. The female is larger than the male, and she has bold orange markings on her front wings. So different are the two sexes that scientists originally classified them as separate species.

Ringlets and their caterpillars feed on grasses. The pretty butterflies are abundant in areas where grass is tall but not dense. The ringlets are especially common near building sites that have been cleared of trees but not yet developed. The butterflies do not frequent farms because they prefer weedy grasses rather than cultivated land, but they do visit gardens located near wild meadows and heathlands.

The ringlet's eyespots serve as decoys to trick a predator, such as a bird, into believing that the butterfly's eyes and body are near the end of the wings. The predator will attack the wingtips, not the ringlet's more vulnerable body. As a result the butterfly is able to escape with minimal damage. At rest the ringlet usually displays its eyespots. But when disturbed, it flies to a new perch, covers its eyespots with its back wings, and turns its body to face the sun. In this position the butterfly makes the best use of its camouflage coloration.

Silver-Washed Fritillary Butterfly
Argynnis paphia

Length: about 1½ inches
Diet: violet leaves (larvae); fruit juices and nectar (adults)
Method of Reproduction: egg layer

Home: Europe, Asia, and northern Africa
Order: Butterflies and moths
Family: Brush-footed butterflies

Cities, Towns, and Farms

Arthropods

© LAURA SIVELL / PAPILIO / CORBIS

The silver-washed fritillary butterfly has several cousins in the United States, including the common silverspot fritillary, *Speyeria diana*, of the southeastern states. Fritillaries are members of the brush-footed butterfly family. These insects are distinctive for their small, nonworking front legs, which resemble little brushes.

Fritillaries are delightfully active butterflies, common wherever wild violets grow. They are about 1½ inches long with many black spots and bands across the wings. Most fritillaries display silvery spots or blotches on the underside of their back wings.

The silver-washed species lives throughout Europe, northern Africa, and across the temperate parts of Asia. It is most abundant in forests, especially in clearings and along the edges of woodlands. This butterfly is most visible in areas inhabited by people in July and August, when it flits among thistle and blackberry bushes, sipping their sweet nectar.

After mating in the summer sunlight, the female lays her eggs in a spiral around a tree trunk or directly on a violet. The caterpillars that hatch are nocturnal. During the day, they hide under the leaves of various violet plants. At dusk, they come out to feed on the violet leaves.

Large Caddisfly
Phryganea sp.

Length: ½ to 1 inch
Diet: aquatic plants (larva)
Home: worldwide in freshwater outside permanently frozen regions

Method of Reproduction: egg layer
Order: Caddisflies
Family: Large caddisflies

 Fresh Water

 Arthropods

© E. R. DEGGINGER / COLOR PIC, INC.

There are more than 4,000 species of caddisfly in the world. All are long, slender, mothlike insects with four delicate, fuzzy wings. The large caddisflies are the biggest of their kind.

Large caddisflies generally rest during the day, while hiding in cool, dark places. At night, they hover above the surface of ponds and marshes. Near civilization, they often swarm around bright lights. After mating within the swarm, females lay their eggs on stones or plants in or near the water.

The larval caddisfly, called a caddisworm, looks like a small caterpillar. The caddisworm lives in marshes and ponds, and breathes through tiny gills. It uses strips of plant material to construct a long, slender tube, or case, around its soft body. In this protective suit of armor, the caddisworm travels in search of plant food. Sometimes it emerges from its case to feed and then retreats indoors again to rest. When the caddisworm is ready to transform into an adult fly, it attaches its tubular case to a solid object, closes the opening, and pupates (passes through the pupal state of development) inside. Once it has grown wings, the creature chews its way out of the case, crawls out of the water, and dries itself on a sunny stone or other object. It has emerged as a beautiful caddisfly.

Spectacled Caiman
Caiman crocodilus

Length: 3½ to 8½ feet
Diet: fish, turtles, and other aquatic vertebrates; also insects
Number of Eggs: 14 to 40

Home: Central and South America; introduced into Florida
Order: Crocodilians
Family: Alligators

   Fresh Water

Reptiles

© THEO ALLOFS / CORBIS

Some people actually buy baby caimans as household pets. Unfortunately, these reptiles grow very quickly and become quite aggressive. Most people eventually decide that they can no longer care for their pet caimans and release them into the wild. If released in a cold climate, the spectacled caiman may die. But if it is returned to the wild in a warm climate, its chance of survival is better. A population of spectacled caimans has been introduced in Florida in precisely this fashion.

This species has an unusual curved ridge of bone between its eyes that makes the caiman look like it is wearing a pair of glasses, or spectacles. Its skin is thick and leathery, and is prized by humans. People have killed millions of spectacled caimans to make pocketbooks and other products from their valuable skin. Consequently, one subspecies, *Caiman crocodilus apaporiensis*, is now endangered.

The spectacled caiman lays up to 40 eggs, many of which are eaten by lizards and other animals. The female caiman builds her nest in a large pile of vegetation. Eggs that survive predators hatch in about 90 days. A newborn caiman feeds on small invertebrates such as snails and aquatic insects. But before long the young caiman is able to catch bigger prey and becomes a source of concern to fish, turtles, and other animals that the caiman finds tasty.

Canvasback
Aythya valisineria

Length: 19 to 24 inches
Weight: up to 3 pounds
Diet: aquatic plants, mollusks, insects, and small fish

Number of Eggs: 7 to 12
Home: North America
Order: Waterfowl
Family: Geese and ducks

Fresh Water

Birds

The canvasback is a diving duck with a sloping forehead and a long, angular black bill. Male canvasbacks have a reddish head; females and ducklings have a brown head. The body is a pale grayish white. People who gave this duck its common name thought that the grayish white body looked like canvas material.

The canvasback lives in the marshes, bays, and large lakes of North America. It migrates in spring and fall, flying high in the sky in V-shaped flocks or in long lines. In the spring, it flies to breeding grounds—some as far north as Alaska. Then, in late fall, it heads south to warmer areas.

Canvasbacks have large webbed feet set far back on the body. They are excellent swimmers and divers, feeding on roots and underwater parts of pondweeds, wild celery, and other aquatic plants. They also strain grass seeds out of the bottom mud and eat small fish, mollusks, and aquatic insects.

The female usually builds her nest among tall reeds in shallow water. It is a large, bulky nest, which is constructed of reeds and dry grass that she gathers nearby. She lines the nest with soft down feathers plucked from her own body. After the female canvasback lays her eggs, she sits on them for about 24 days, until the young birds hatch. The ducklings are yellowish olive–green at birth and can swim soon after hatching.

Brown Capuchin
Cebus apella

Length of the Body: 13 to 22 inches
Length of the Tail: 16 to 20 inches
Diet: fruits, insects, and small animals

Weight: 5½ to 7½ pounds
Number of Young: 1
Home: South America
Order: Primates
Family: New World monkeys
Subfamily: True capuchins

  Rain forests

Mammals

© DOUG CHEESEMAN / PETER ARNOLD, INC.

This bright, lively capuchin is also called the hooded capuchin because of the black skullcap of stiff hairs on its head. Its long, furry tail is prehensile, which means it can be used like a fifth hand. The capuchin uses its tail as a safety rope when it travels through the treetops.

As a newborn, a brown capuchin is quite helpless, clinging to its mother and nursing. The baby's older siblings, especially its sisters, show great interest in the newest family member. In about three months—when the newborn becomes a toddler—it returns its siblings' affection and tries to play with them. Over the next few months, the youngster begins to play with other capuchin children its age. It also finds a favorite adult male to spend time with—a father figure, so to speak.

Young capuchin males and females tend to play separately. The young males spend a lot of time play-fighting. The young females often join in the roughhousing. But as they grow older, the female capuchins spend more time sitting quietly together grooming each other, like teenagers fixing each other's hair. However, capuchin females are quite liberated by human standards. In this species, it is the female who woos the male. Biologists say that a female capuchin will boldly choose a male and beckon him to follow with gestures and sweet cooing sounds. Male capuchins often remain uninterested in courting.

Capybara
Hydrochaeris hydrochaeris

Length of the Body: 3⅓ to 4⅓ feet
Weight: 110 to 154 pounds
Diet: grasses and water plants

Number of Young: 3 or 4
Home: South America
Order: Rodents
Family: Capybaras

 Grasslands

 Mammals

© KEVIN SCHAFER / CORBIS

More than twice the size of a jackrabbit, the capybara is the largest rodent in the world. Not surprisingly, people hunt the stout capybara for its meat. In some places, ranchers kill the creature solely because it competes with cows and sheep for grass. As a result of overhunting, capybaras have nearly disappeared in parts of their range. Some countries, like Venezuela, have begun protecting the animal, as well as breeding it in captivity.

Capybaras are also known as water hogs. As the name suggests, they are usually found near swamps and water holes. The water provides a refuge from the midday heat. Capybaras are excellent swimmers. Their eyes and ears are positioned high on the head, so they can see and hear easily while swimming. Capybaras also have webbing between their fingers and toes, which helps them paddle. When frightened, they can remain underwater for several minutes.

During the dry season—when water holes are few and far between—as many as 30 to 50 capybaras may gather around a single mud puddle. When the rains arrive, the animals break off into smaller groups. Typically, each family group includes one adult male and one or more females, with their young. Bachelor males often band together in separate groups. Each day the capybara troops must travel long distances in search of food. Yet they nearly always return to the same spot at night.

13

Grass Carp (White Amur)
Ctenopharyngodon idella

Length: up to 49 inches
Weight: up to 23 pounds
Diet: plants
Home: native to Southeast Asia; introduced to the United States

Method of Reproduction: egg layer
Order: Carps and their relatives
Family: Carps

  Fresh Water

Fish

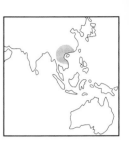

© GERARD LACZ / PETER ARNOLD, INC.

In the 1920s scientists discovered the grass carp in Hunan, China. At the time the Hunan people were selling it in great quantities on their city streets. People loved the taste of this meaty fish. The grass carp is remarkable for its very broad head and large scales. It lacks the barbels, or "whiskers," seen on other carp.

This carp has a voracious appetite for weeds. It can extend its upper lip and jaw forward, helping it pull great quantities of vegetation from the lake beds. Grass carp are also amazingly adaptable and can survive in a wide range of water temperatures.

In the 1960s game officials in the United States thought that this fish could help them clean up their overgrown lakes and ponds. As a result, grass carp now live in the waters of at least 34 states. Unfortunately, the carp's introduction to the United States may have been unwise. Biologists now realize that many native fish and waterbirds depend on aquatic vegetation. The grass carp steals their food. And lack of vegetation deprives the water of oxygen. In most states, it is now illegal to introduce unsterile grass carp to any lake. Still, there are at least 115 lakes and reservoirs currently stocked with the fish, and several hatcheries in North Carolina continue to breed the carp. Only time will tell if the introduction of this fish was a help or a hazard.

Australian Cassowary
Casuarius casuarius

Height: 4 to 5 feet
Diet: fruits, seeds, berries, and snails
Number of Eggs: 3 to 5
Length of the Egg: 5 to 6 inches

Top Speed: 30 miles per hour
Home: Australia, New Guinea, and nearby islands
Order: Emus and cassowaries
Family: Cassowaries

 Forests and Mountains

 Birds

© HANS & JUDY BESTE / ANIMALS ANIMALS / EARTH SCENES

The name *cassowary* is Papuan (the language spoken by people on the island of New Guinea) for "horned head" and refers to this bird's bony helmetlike crest. Biologists suspect that Australian cassowaries need their "helmets" for protection as they crash through tangles of shrubs and vines. These large, flightless birds recklessly run through the deepest, thickest part of the Australian forest at speeds of up to 30 miles per hour!

The cassowary is one of the few birds in the world that has been known to kill humans. When cornered, it will kick with its powerful legs, injuring its enemy with deadly sharp claws. Fortunately, it is a very shy creature and will try desperately to avoid people.

Mated Australian cassowary couples build large nests of sticks and leaves. It is the father cassowary that sits on the eggs, which hatch one by one. Both parents help to care for the chicks. The family may remain together even after the young have grown. Cassowary families require large areas of land to survive. Their appetites are so great that they quickly strip all the food from any one area and must constantly move to find more food.

Cassowaries somewhat resemble ostriches, which are large, flightless birds found in Africa. But biologists are not sure whether these two types of birds are actually related or have different ancestors.

Turkestan Desert Cat
Felis thinobia

Length of the Body: 18 to 22 inches
Length of the Tail: 11 to 13½ inches
Diet: lizards, small rodents, and birds

Weight: 4½ to 8 pounds
Number of Young: 2 to 4
Home: Asia
Order: Carnivores
Family: Cats

 Deserts

 Mammals

© ROD WILLIAMS / BRUCE COLEMAN INC.

The Turkestan desert cat lives among the sand dunes in the deserts of Central Asia. About the size of a large domestic cat, its long hair makes it appear much bigger. Like other Old World wild cats, this is a rare and mysterious creature. It has never been studied in the wild, so no one knows whether or not the Turkestan desert cat is in danger of extinction.

This cat is recognized by its broad skull and its large, wide ears, which are set far apart on the head. Scientists believe that the naked inner surfaces of the cat's large ears help cool the animal's body by dissipating heat. Large, widely separated ears also help the cat hear faint noises in the dark of night. Like many desert animals, this cat is nocturnal. Thick cushions of long hair protect the cat's feet from the hot desert sand. These foot cushions also act like snowshoes, preventing the cat from sinking into the sand.

A few Turkestan desert cats have been raised successfully in zoos. They require a deep layer of sand in their enclosures. After a meal the cat buries its leftovers in the sand and retrieves them later when it is hungry again. From captive Turkestan cats, we know that females give birth approximately two months after mating. The kittens are boldly striped, but the stripes gradually fade as the cats mature into yellowish-gray adults.

Eastern Tent Caterpillar
Malacosoma americanum

Length: 3 inches (larva)
Wingspan: 1 to 2 inches (adult)
Method of Reproduction: egg layer

Diet: leaves and buds
Number of Eggs: 150 to 200
Home: eastern North America
Order: Butterflies and moths
Family: Moths

 Forests and Mountains

 Arthropods

© GARY W. CARTER / CORBIS

The eastern tent caterpillar is actually the larval form of the common North American moth *Malacosoma americanum*. In the case of the tent caterpillar, however, the larval form, or caterpillar, is of particular importance to scientists, gardeners, and tree lovers. That is because every year, tent caterpillars go on an eating rampage, devouring the leaves and buds on millions of trees and shrubs, causing great damage.

The damage cycle begins in early spring, when the female moth deposits up to 200 eggs on the twigs of a plant. The eggs hatch about the time the first leaves begin to appear. The larvae immediately begin feeding on the leaves and buds. The larvae also build a characteristic silken nest, or tent, in a fork of the tree or shrub. They do not feed within the tent, but move to nearby branches looking for food. As they creep along, the caterpillars spin a silken thread that is later used to find their way home to the tent. It is during this stage that tent caterpillars can succeed in eating every leaf and bud off a tree.

About four to eight weeks after hatching, the larvae reach maturity and pupate. The mature larvae, about 3 inches long, have dark, rather hairy bodies, The adults emerge in the second half of the summer. They are drab brown moths with wingspans averaging 1 to 2 inches.

Stone Centipede
Lithobius forficatus

Length: up to 1 inch
Diet: small insects
Method of Reproduction: egg layer

Home: Eurasia
Order: Lithobiomorphs
Family: Lithobids

 Forests and Mountains

 Arthropods

© BILL BEATTY / ANIMALS ANIMALS / EARTH SCENES

With 15 pairs of legs, the adult stone centipede can spare a few. Its first pair of legs is not used for walking at all. They have evolved into poisonous jaws, and the stone centipede uses them to bite and kill its prey. The stone centipede's back legs break off easily. This is a handy trick if an enemy, such as a mouse, bites the centipede from behind. The legs simply pop off in the mouse's mouth, allowing the centipede to escape. When a leg breaks, muscles at the top of the limb close around the wound. This prevents the centipede from bleeding to death. The injured centipede will grow a new leg the next time it sheds its skin.

Stone centipedes breed in early spring. After mating, the female lays her eggs, one at a time. She picks up each egg with a claw near her tail and carries the egg to an area where she can roll it in dirt. By covering her eggs with soil particles, the female disguises them from predators, as well as from her mate. Male centipedes will eat the eggs if they can find them.

When they are born, stone centipedes have only seven pairs of legs. During their first year of life, the young centipedes change shape, or metamorphose, four times. With each transformation, they gain a few legs. Stone centipedes may live to be three years old. As their name implies, they make their homes under stones, as well as rotting wood and fallen leaves.

Veiled Chameleon
Chamaeleo calyptratus

Length: about 15 inches
Weight: about 8 ounces
Diet: insects

Home: Yemen
Order: Lizards and snakes
Family: Chameleons

 Grasslands

 Reptiles

© DAVID A. NORTHCOTT / CORBIS

Veiled chameleons have been called the perfect "party animals." The male of this species grows his own fantastic party hat when he is about six months old. But, in truth, the chameleon is anything but social.

You can tell when a male veiled chameleon is angry, because his head cone flushes a bright turquoise green, and vivid stripes and spots appear on the rest of his body. Usually this display is enough to frighten an intruder away. But the veiled chameleon will also use its muscular tail to lash out at an enemy. When all else fails, it will bite—hard!

A veiled chameleon also displays its colors to attract a mate. When not excited, it wears a camouflage pattern of dull green and blue. These colors blend in perfectly with the leaves of the acacia trees in which the lizards live. The veiled chameleon spends most of its time lying in ambush for unsuspecting insects. The chameleon snags its prey with a long tongue, some 10 to 15 inches long. At the end of the tongue is a sticky pad that works like flypaper.

The acacia scrublands where the veiled chameleon lives are hot and dry. Daytime temperatures are often over 100°F, and less than 1 inch of rain falls in the average year. The veiled chameleon survives by drinking the small amount of moisture that blows in from the ocean and condenses on the leaves of the acacia.

Cherubfish
Centropyge argi

Home: Caribbean Sea, Gulf of Mexico, and Atlantic Ocean around Florida, Bermuda, and Bahamas
Length: up to 2¾ inches

Diet: algae
Number of Eggs: about 200
Order: Perchlike fishes
Family: Butterflyfishes

 Oceans and Shores

 Fish

© MARK SMITH / PHOTO RESEARCHERS

The cherubfish is a small, round, rosy-faced angelfish. Notice the bright blue eye ring on its yellowish-pink head. The rest of the body is always a matching shade of blue, which darkens as the cherubfish ages. Like other angelfish, this species has a pancake-flat body. There are several small spines beneath the eyes and gill covers.

The cherubfish is one of a group known as pygmy angelfish. This particular species is seldom seen and may be rare. It lives more than 50 feet deep, in the dark recesses of underwater cliffs and coral reefs. And it is a busy fish, darting back and forth while searching for food. Although cherubfish are generally curious and fearless of scuba divers, they can make a hasty retreat when threatened. As a result, they are very difficult to spear by divers. Female cherubfish have the fascinating ability to change sex when males are in shorty supply. If the male dies or is removed from an aquarium, the largest, most dominant female takes his place. She begins acting like a male almost immediately; the physical sex change takes about 20 days.

Cherubfish spawn at dusk, with the male pursuing one female at a time. The pair start by nuzzling and fluttering around one another in deep water. Then they begin a slow, spiraling ascent, releasing their sperm and eggs at the top of their spiral.

Ramirez' Dwarf Cichlid
Apistogramma ramirezi

Length: up to 2 inches
Diet: insects and small invertebrates
Number of Eggs: 150 to 200

Home: Venezuela
Order: Perchlike fishes
Family: Cichlids

 Fresh Water

 Fish

© JEAN-MICHEL LABAT / JACANA / PHOTO RESEARCHERS

Cichlids are a large family of tropical fish found in the rivers and lakes of Central and South America. In appearance, they resemble the sunfish of North America, and, like sunfish, some large cichlids are important sources of food. Smaller species, such as the Ramirez' dwarf cichlid, are popular aquarium pets.

The Ramirez' dwarf cichlid may be the most beautiful of all the cichlids. The male, considerably more brilliant than his mate, is a delicate crimson, with flanks that reflect a rainbow of hues. This species can always be recognized by a dark spot under the dorsal fin (the fin on the back).

Ramirez' dwarf cichlids live no more than two years. Yet, in that time, they can produce thousands of offspring. With no set mating season, this species spawns several times a year, producing up to 200 young in each brood.

Before they mate, the male and female Ramirez' dwarf cichlid clean a small patch of mud on the bottom of a lake or river and dig a little pit. After the female lays her eggs in this nest, her mate fertilizes them. The eggs hatch in two to five days, and both parents take turns guarding the newborns. For the first four to six days of their lives, the baby cichlids feed off the yolk sacs from their eggs, which remain attached to their bellies. They remain with their mother for up to a month before swimming away on their own.

Rio Grande Cichlid
Cichlasoma cyanoguttatum

Diet: plants, decaying matter, and occasionally small snails and fish

Method of Reproduction: egg layer

Length: up to 12 inches

Home: native to Texas and Mexico; introduced to Florida

Order: Perchlike fishes

Family: Cichlids

 Fresh Water

 Fish

© HANS REINHARD / BRUCE COLEMAN INC.

Cichlids make up a large family of mainly tropical freshwater fish including the angelfish, a popular aquarium pet. The Rio Grande cichlid is the northernmost representative of this family and the only cichlid native to the United States. It is an exceptionally attractive fish, especially the male, which is often larger and more brilliant than his mate. Adults have sparkling sky-blue or sea-green spots or wavy stripes. Young Rio Grande cichlids have a clay-colored body with dark bands and blotches. These intelligent fish are excellent aquarium pets. In fact, owners say they can recognize the cichlids' individual personalities.

Originally Rio Grande cichlids lived only in the rivers and pools that emptied into the lower Rio Grande in southern Texas and northeastern Mexico. Recently people have successfully introduced this beautiful fish to rivers in central Texas and Florida.

Rio Grande cichlids spawn in large nesting communities, usually in the deepest parts of rivers and spring-fed pools. The species' diet varies according to where the fish live. In central Texas the cichlids are primarily plant eaters. In southern Texas they eat both plant and animal matter. In Mexico they feed on dead animal matter, as well as on snails and small fish. These dietary differences reflect both the availability of food in each area and the needs of other fish species, which compete for the food.

Clione
Clione limacina

Length: up to 1½ inches
Diet: smaller sea snails
Method of Reproduction: egg layer

Home: northern oceans
Order: Gymnosomates
Family: Clioniids

 Oceans and Shores

Other Invertebrates

© FLIP NICKLIN / MINDEN PICTURES

The pale-blue clione seems to fly through the water as it swims near the surface of the sea. Its name comes from the Latin word *clio*, which means "sea nymph," or "sea fairy." The clione is also called the naked sea butterfly. A clione is "naked" because it is a sea snail without a shell. Like an underwater butterfly, it moves through the water by flapping two thin, broad fins. These winglike fins grow from the front of the clione's muscular foot. Its head bears two almost transparent tentacles.

Despite its delicate appearance, the clione is a fearsome predator. It eats smaller sea snails, which it catches in an amazing way. Growing inside the clione's stomach are a variety of hunting weapons: sticky tentacles, suckered arms, and sacks covered with tiny hooks. The clione pushes these weapons out of its mouth and attacks. Once it has grabbed hold of a victim, the clione pulls its meal into its stomach. The clione, in turn, is eaten by the gigantic right whale, which can swallow hundreds in a single gulp. Fortunately, these tiny sea snails are very abundant throughout the cool northern oceans.

When it is time to mate, the female clione squirts clumps of eggs into the water. There are about 25 eggs in each of her clumps. At the same time, nearby males squirt their sperm into the water, fertilizing the eggs.

Spitting Cobra
Naja nigricollis

Length: average 5 feet, but up to 9 feet

Diet: mammals, birds, eggs, other snakes, lizards, and frogs

Number of Eggs: up to 50

Home: central Africa

Order: Lizards and snakes

Family: Cobras and their relatives

 Grasslands

 Reptiles

© ANTHONY BANNISTER / NHPA

Like all cobras, this species will bite to defend itself. But it prefers to spit its venom and then quickly escape. The snake aims its poisonous spray at its enemy's face. The venom comes out of the spitting cobra's mouth in two jet streams. The jets widen into a broad spray that can reach 10 to 12 feet. If it gets into the eyes, the cobra's venom can cause great pain and perhaps even blindness. Venom that falls on unbroken skin does no harm.

Oddly, the fearsome spitting cobra often prefers to "play dead" rather than fight. The cobra simply lies limp against the ground, as if dead, until danger has passed. It then silently glides away.

Spitting cobras tend to sleep through the day and come out to hunt at night. They usually adopt a tree hole or a rodent burrow for their daytime home. The adult female lays her eggs there and then wraps her body around them for warmth. When the eggs hatch, the newborns are 10 to 12 inches long and ready to spit venom. The baby snakes often feed on insects, graduating to larger animals as they get older.

Some people actually enjoy keeping spitting cobras as pets. With good care the snakes lose their spitting habit and may even take dead rats from their owner's hand. Once tamed, spitting cobras will breed in captivity and may live up to 22 years.

Andean Cock-of-the-Rock
Rupicola peruviana

Length: 11 to 12 inches
Home: Venezuela, Colombia, Ecuador, Peru, and Bolivia
Diet: fruit and insects

Number of Eggs: 2
Order: Perching birds
Family: Cotingas

 Forests and Mountains

 Birds

© KEVIN SCHAFER / CORBIS

The Andean cock-of-the-rock lives in the forests of northwest South America. It lives at altitudes from 1,650 to 7,500 feet in rocky areas close to a stream or a river. Many of these birds live near the sources of the Orinoco and Amazon rivers. They have brightly colored feathers and eat berries, fruit, and insects that they find in abundance in the rich tropical forests.

The males put on a wild show at mating time. In front of the watching females, several males perform acrobatic dances. They jump in place, spin around, and strut about while spreading their black tails, which contrast with their bright orange bodies. They bow, step in all directions, and scratch the ground. Then they jump up and down at a rhythmic pace. When they are finished, they chirp and fly off to let another male take over. Eventually couples form as each female chooses her favorite star.

The cock-of-the-rock settles in small colonies and builds a strong nest made of plants mixed with mud. It attaches the nest to the side of a rock over a stream or in a cave. The female sits on the two eggs she lays for about one month. When the chicks hatch, the male helps feed and raise them.

Indians who live in the forests of South America hunt the cock-of-the-rock because they eat its meat. They also use the brightly colored feathers to decorate their clothes.

Malayan Colugo
Cynocephalus variegatus

Length of the Body: 13 to 17 inches
Length of the Tail: 9 to 11 inches
Weight: 2 to 3 ¾ pounds
Diet: mainly leaves; also buds, flowers, and fruits

Number of Young: 1
Home: Malaysia
Order: Flying lemurs, or colugos
Family: Flying lemurs, or colugos

 Rain forests

 Mammals

© PETER HARD / BRUCE COLEMAN INC.

When its arms and legs are outstretched, the Malayan colugo, or flying lemur, becomes a living kite. It glides from tree to tree using large folds of skin that stretch between its neck, arms, legs, and tail. This large, furry membrane is called a "patagium." A few other mammals, such as the flying squirrel, have similar patagia. But none is as large or as effective as the colugo's. The colugo's flying web even extends between its fingers. The animal can steer its flight by moving its tail like a rudder.

The Malayan colugo spends its entire life high in the trees of the rainforest, never dropping to the ground except by accident. Yet this tree creature is not a very good climber. The large folds of skin between its limbs interfere with its movement.

The colugo gives birth to only one baby at a time. To carry her infant, the mother hangs upside down like a sloth, with the baby on her belly and cradled in her patagium. The newborn is exceptionally tiny and helpless. For its first few weeks of life, it can do little but nurse at its mother's breast.

The colugo's only predator is the human hunter. Fortunately for the Malayan colugo, its speckled fur is excellent camouflage against tree bark. However, humans continue to cut down the rain forest at a rapid rate, threatening the survival of these and countless other precious species.

European Coot
Fulica atra

Length: 15 inches
Diet: aquatic plants, mollusks, worms, insects, fish, and fish eggs
Number of Eggs: 6 to 9
Egg Length: 2 inches

Home: Europe, Asia, Africa, and Australia
Order: Rails, coots, cranes, and others
Family: Rails, gallinules, and coots

 Fresh Water

 Birds

© ROGER WILMSHURST / PHOTO RESEARCHERS

At first glance, you might mistake the European coot for a duck. Like its relative the American coot, it has webbed feet, acts rather like a duck, and often swims with flocks of ducks. You can tell the difference between a coot and duck by looking at their backs. A duck's back is flat, while the coot's is elegantly curved. You can also recognize a coot by the commotion it makes when taking off from the water. It starts by swimming faster and faster until it is literally running across the surface of the water. A coot can run like this for several yards, making loud splashes with its flat feet, before finally lifting into the air. As you might have guessed from its awkward takeoff, the coot is not a strong flier.

Coots will live only in a lake or pond covered with floating plants and reeds. They spend time swimming beneath these plants, chasing fish, and rooting around for insects.

Male and female coots build elaborate nests that rise about a foot above the water. These platforms are hidden among the tall water plants. The female coot lays her eggs in March. She and her mate take turns sitting on them. Both parents help to care for the chicks. They lead them into the water in the morning to search for food and back to the nest at night for warmth. The parents catch food for their chicks for the first month and continue protecting them for another month after that.

Great Cormorant
Phalacrocorax carbo

Length: 30 to 40 inches
Wingspan: 50 to 63 inches
Weight: 5 to 11 pounds
Diet: fish
Number of Eggs: 4 to 6

Home: bodies of fresh water and coastal areas in many parts of the world
Order: Pelicans and gannets
Family: Cormorants and shags

 Oceans and Shores

 Birds

For such a large bird, the great cormorant is rarely seen by people. The reason may lie with the bird's tendency to avoid places where people live: the great cormorant feels most comfortable on cliffs, remote islands, and along the banks and coasts of rivers and lakes. Another possible explanation for the rare sightings is the great cormorant's coloration: usually entirely black, including its legs and webbed feet. Whatever the reason, the great cormorant holds the distinction of being the largest of its species in North America.

True bird lovers who seek out the great cormorant sometimes find it perched on a rock or a buoy with its wings spread. Unlike many birds that feed on fish, the great cormorant does not have waterproof wings, and it must put aside time now and again to dry them thoroughly. Only the luckiest bird-watchers happen upon a cormorant on the hunt. This great bird eats almost exclusively fish. When a particularly tasty fish catches a cormorant's fancy, the bird holds its wings close to its body and, steering itself with its feet, propels itself underwater after the prey.

More often than not, the cormorant catches the fish in its large, hooked bill and brings it to the surface. Before dining, however, the cormorant cleans the fish by shaking it and tossing it about in the air. Then the cormorant swallows the fish whole.

White-Browed Coucal
Centropus superciliosus

Length: about 16 inches
Weight: about 5⅓ ounces
Home: eastern and Central Africa
Diet: mainly large insects

Number of Eggs: 3 to 5
Order: Cuckoos, turacos, and hoatzins
Family: Cuckoos

 Grasslands

 Birds

© WINIFRED WISNIEWSKI / FRANK LANE PICTURE AGENCY / CORBIS

Coucals are large, long-tailed cuckoos with brown and black feathers. The name *coucal* derives from the French words that mean "lark-cuckoo," and refers to this bird's bubbly, larklike call. The coucal sings an especially distinctive song, which sounds like liquid being poured from a glass bottle. In fact, the people of eastern Africa often refer to the coucal as "the water-bottle bird."

The white-browed coucal has wide white "eyebrows" over each eye. Its dark brown feathers are streaked in creamy white across the face and neck. Like many coucals, the eyes of this species are large and blood red. Although the bird belongs to the cuckoo family, it more closely resembles the

pheasant. Heavily built and rather clumsy in flight, the coucal spends most of its life on the ground.

While most coucals live in swamps and marshes, the white-browed species prefers Africa's dry savanna and bush country. It spends the day hidden among tall grasses, hunting for tasty, large insects. When flushed from cover, the bird flounders through the air like a poor swimmer struggling through water. Although awkward in flight, the coucal often lands on a low tree and then nimbly jumps from branch to branch. These birds nest in low bushes or on the ground, hidden among underbrush. The nest is usually a rounded dome, which the female weaves from grasses.

Common Land Crab
Gecarcinus ruricola

Width of the Shell: about 3½ inches
Diet: mainly fruits; also a wide variety of plant and animal matter
Method of Reproduction: egg layer

Home: southern Florida, Bahamas, and West Indies
Order: Shrimps, crabs, and lobsters
Family: Land crabs

 Forests and Mountains

 Arthropods

© JEAN-BERNARD CARILLET / LONELY PLANET IMAGES

Unlike most crabs, the adult black land crab often lives far from the ocean. In its travels inland, it can climb mountains several hundred feet above sea level. During the May rainy season, females return to the sea to release their young. Years ago, many thousands of these crabs tumbled down the hillsides each spring. In their rush to the sea, they would even march through open doors and windows. The crab is not as plentiful today, although it is still common in the Bahamas.

After mating in early spring, the female black land crab places her eggs under her shell for safekeeping. She migrates to the ocean just before the eggs are ready to hatch. As the mother stands in shallow water, the tiny newborn pop out and drift away with the tide. In the open ocean, they float among the plankton. They must undergo several body changes before they are ready to come ashore.

Unlike other types of land crabs, this species does not dig burrows. Adults avoid the drying sun by living on shady mountainsides. During the day, they rest in moist rock crevices and under leaf litter. Small, young crabs live closer to the sea and spend the day hidden under stones along beaches. Both young and old come out after dark. They are especially fond of fruits, but nibble on just about anything, from driftwood to dead animals.

European Edible Crab
Cancer pagurus

Diameter of the Shell: up to 12 inches

Diet: snails and other small animals

Method of Reproduction: egg layer

Weight: up to 13 pounds

Home: coastal waters of Europe

Order: Lobsters, shrimp, and crabs

Family: Cancrid crabs

 Oceans and Shores

 Arthropods

© STEPHEN DALTON / PHOTO RESEARCHERS

The most noticeable feature of the European edible crab is its front legs. These legs are greatly enlarged and end in big claws. The crab uses the claws to hold food, defend itself, and to communicate with other crabs. If the crab loses one of the claws, it can grow a new one.

Like other crabs, the body of the European edible variety has three sections: head, thorax, and abdomen. The abdomen is small and folded under the thorax. Each section has several pairs of jointed appendages. On the head are two pairs of antennae, which are used for feeling and smelling. On the thorax are five pairs of legs. The abdomen has small appendages called swimmerets. These are not used for swimming. The male uses his swimmerets during mating. The female carries her eggs on her swimmerets.

The European edible crab's body is protected by a broad, flattened shell called a carapace. The shell is much wider than it is long. The shell does not grow; rather, as the crab grows, it must shed, or molt, its shell. Underneath is a new body covering that soon hardens. But for a day or two after molting, the crab is quite soft and easy prey for other animals.

Edible crabs are an important source of human food. They also play an important role in food chains in coastal waters. As scavengers along the sea bottom, they rid the environment of dead plants and animals.

Spider Crab
Pugettia gracilis

Width of the Shell: about 1½ inches (male); about 1 inch (female)
Diet: kelp
Number of Eggs: 6,000 to 13,000

Home: Pacific Ocean off the West Coast of North America
Order: Shrimps, crabs, and lobsters
Family: Majid crabs

 Oceans and Shores

 Arthropods

© JEFF FOOT / BRUCE COLEMAN INC.

The spider crab is at home in the shallow, rocky waters off the Pacific coast of North America. There it scrambles daintily across floating beds of eelgrass and kelp. Its smooth, rapid movements have earned it the nickname "graceful kelp crab." Spider crabs feed on small bits of kelp, which they snip with their tiny claws. The crabs in turn are food for seals and sea otters, which also live among the kelp beds.

To hide from its enemies, the spider crab changes its colors to match the surroundings. A spider crab in eelgrass, for example, may be green, while those on kelp may be brown. However, the spider crab is not a quick-change artist. A total color change can be completed only when the crab sheds its old skin, a process called molting. Like most crustaceans, the spider crab has a hard, stiff covering of skin called an exoskeleton, or "outer skeleton." Periodically the crab outgrows and discards its old skin. A newly molted crab is soft and defenseless until its new skin hardens. However, it is only in this "naked" state that the crab can mate.

Spider crabs breed year round. After mating, the female tucks her fertilized eggs under her belly. She carries them until they hatch into tiny, free-swimming larvae. The larvae feed on the microscopic food that floats through the ocean. They soon settle onto kelp or eelgrass and transform into adults.

South African Crowned Crane
Balearica regulorum

Height: about 3½ feet
Weight: about 8¼ pounds
Diet: insects, fish, frogs, seeds, and plants
Number of Eggs: usually 2

Home: Central and southern Africa
Order: Cranes and rails
Family: Cranes

 Fresh Water

 Birds

© KENNAN WARD / CORBIS

The spectacular crowned crane of South Africa appears to be dressed for a fancy costume ball. This is close to the truth—the crane is indeed dressed for a showy dance. In mating season, males and females perform spectacular courtship displays. They jump into the air, spread their wings, and dance about excitedly. As with other cranes, both sexes are equally beautiful, with showy feathers and elegant coloration. The crowned crane is particularly famous for its bristly crest of straw-colored head feathers.

Most South African crowned cranes live near the edges of swamps. Outside of breeding season, they gather in large family groups. Together, they wade through shallow water, eating a variety of animal and plant matter. After the African rainy season, the groups split into mated pairs. Each couple build a nest by stamping down tall marsh reeds and pushing them into a heap. On this mound the female lays two pale-blue eggs, about 3¼ inches long and 2½ inches wide. Soon after the chicks hatch, their parents lead them to water and teach them how to hunt.

At one time, this crane was common. Unfortunately, it has become scarce because much of its natural habitat has been polluted or destroyed. As towns and industries expand, people drain swamps for water or fill them in to make way for construction. Adding to the crane's troubles, people steal the bird's young for fancy pets.

Brown Creeper
Certhia familiaris

Length: 5 to 6 inches
Diet: insects
Home: North and Central
  America, Europe, and Asia

Number of Eggs: 5 to 6
Order: Perching birds
Family: Tree creepers
Suborder: Songbirds

 Forests and Mountains

Birds

© STEVE MASLOWSKI / PHOTO RESEARCHERS

The tiny brown creeper spends its day climbing up one tree trunk after another, searching for tasty insects. Nature has equipped the bird well for tree climbing: its sharp claws enable it to cling close to the bark, and its strong, stiff tail acts as a brace, or prop, to keep the bird from sliding backward. Also notice the brown creeper's long, thin, downward-curving bill. It is perfect for probing tiny insect holes

This nervous little bird is easily frightened. But when left undisturbed, it slowly and carefully probes every inch of a tree's bark for insects. The brown creeper starts at the bottom of a tree trunk and gradually works its way to the top in a perfect spiral—not missing an inch of bark with its diligent probing. Once at the top of one tree, the creeper flies to the bottom of the next. Again it works it way, round and round the tree trunk, to the top. Occasionally the brown creeper pauses from its work to sing a sweet, light melody: "Trees-trees-trees-see-the-trees," it seems to say.

So tiny is the brown creeper that it can tuck its nest behind a bit of loose tree bark. It lines this small crevice with bits of moss and a few of its own feathers. There the female sits on her clutch of eggs. If she has a helpful mate, he may bring her something to eat from time to time or take an occasional turn warming their eggs.

Red-Banded Crevice Creeper

Phrynomerus bifasciatus

Length: 2 to 3¼ inches
Diet: ants and other insects
Number of Eggs: 400 to 1,500

Home: southern Africa
Order: Frogs and toads
Family: Phrynomerids

 Fresh Water

Amphibians

© JANE BURTON / BRUCE COLEMAN INC.

The red-banded crevice creeper wears bright markings on its back as a warning to enemies: its skin produces a foul-smelling, irritating liquid that burns the skin of animals that attempt to bite the frog or people who attempt to pick it up. If a predator eats a crevice creeper, death will likely follow. Fortunately for them, most animals quickly spit out this painful mouthful.

The red-banded crevice creeper has another way to protect itself from predators: it has an unusual ability to turn its head from side to side to change its view. Most other frogs must move their entire body to do this. True to its name, this frog generally avoids open ground by hiding in cracks and

crevices. At night it becomes very active, scrambling about on rocks and in trees. But at dawn the crevice creeper disappears into underground burrows. It often digs itself into termite mounds, which also provide a favorite food.

When the weather is especially dry, the frogs remain in their burrows for days, sometimes weeks, at a time. During the rainy season, they gather in shallow ponds and pools to mate. The male finds a mate by calling out loudly, usually after a heavy rainfall. The receptive female lays her eggs in large, jellylike clumps. She attaches them to underwater plants or drops them onto the bottom of a pond.

Wall Creeper

Tichodroma muraria

Length: 6¼ inches
Diet: insects and their larvae; also spiders and centipedes
Number of Eggs: usually 3

Home: Europe and Central Asia
Order: Perching birds
Family: Nuthatches

 Forests and Mountains

 Birds

© ERIC SODER / NHPA

The wall creeper seems like a dull bird, and, judging by its drab-looking plumage, many people think it is. But when this bird chooses to spread its wings, it exposes lovely red bands of color. When the wall creeper opens its bill, it lets forth an unexpectedly lovely song.

This bird is aptly named; it spends much of its time climbing on rock walls and cliffs. The wall creeper prefers rock that is partly covered with plants, although it often visits stone buildings in mountain villages, especially during winter. The wall creeper always seems to be in motion, flicking its wings and poking its head into wall crevices to find tasty insects and other food. Its long, curved bill is a useful tool for reaching those hard-to-peck-at insects inside cracks and crevices.

During most of the year, the wall creeper lives alone. It joins others only to mate and to raise young. When courting time nears, the male performs an entertaining dance to impress a female. He circles around her with his wings spread and his tail vibrating up and down. At the same time, he rapidly moves his head back and forth.

Wall creepers nest in rock cavities, using grasses and mosses to build cup-shaped nests lined with hair and feathers. The female incubates the eggs for 18 days, but once they hatch, both parents help care for the young birds. The babies learn to fly when they are about three weeks old.

American Crocodile
Crocodylus acutus

Diet: fish, turtles, birds, and mammals
Home: southern Florida, the Caribbean, Central America, and northern South America

Length: up to 21 feet
Number of Eggs: about 30
Order: Crocodilians
Family: Crocodiles

  Fresh Water

Reptiles

 Endangered Animals

© M. H. SHARP / PHOTO RESEARCHERS

American crocodiles are at home in both fresh water and salt water. They are excellent swimmers, using their strong tails to move quickly through the water. They catch prey with their powerful jaws and eat insects, fish, frogs, turtles, birds, and mammals. Attacks on humans are rare, but they do occur. Most crocodiles hunt at night. During the day, they float near the surface, often with their mouths open. When a crocodile closes its mouth, two large teeth remain visible. These two teeth protrude upward, one on either side of the lower jaw. Alligators do not have teeth that protrude when the mouth is closed.

On land, crocodiles appear clumsy. Usually they move slowly. But when they feel threatened or when they are hunting, they can move very fast. They cannot move well from side to side, however. An animal being chased by a crocodile can usually escape by quickly changing its direction. When crocodiles reach maturity, their only real enemies are people who hunt them for their leathery skin and for sport. These reptiles are close to extinction in some areas of the world.

After mating, the female crocodile digs a hole in which to lay her eggs. She piles grass and other matter on top of the eggs. She guards the nest for about three months, until the young crocodiles hatch. Then she carries the young down to the water.

Eurasian Cuckoo
Cuculus canorus

Length: 13 to 15 inches
Weight: about 4 ounces
Diet: caterpillars and other large insects
Number of Eggs: 8 to 12

Home: Europe, Asia, and Africa
Order: Cuckoos, turacos, and hoatzins
Family: Cuckoos

 Forests and Mountains

 Birds

© DAVID KJAER / NATURE PICTURE LIBRARY

Throughout Europe and northern Asia, the cuckoo's familiar song (which sounds like its name) announces the start of spring. This slim, long-tailed bird spends the winter in tropical Africa and southern Asia, and flies north to breed. Most Eurasian cuckoos are slate gray as adults, although a few females remain reddish-brown like their immature young.

After mating in early May, the female cuckoo establishes a large territory. Within it, she locates the nests of smaller perching birds and deposits one egg in each. Cuckoos do not raise their own chicks. Instead, they leave them to be cared for by other birds. Typically each female is attracted to the nest of a specific species, such as a wagtail or a redstart. She may even select the type of nest in which she was raised. The cuckoo must be sly in placing her eggs. If the host bird recognizes the cuckoo egg, it may try to remove the intruder or abandon the nest entirely.

Once in place, the egg develops quickly, hatching in less than two weeks. The chick, larger and bolder than its foster brothers and sisters, often shoves its "siblings" from the nest. One way or another, it usually succeeds in demanding all its parents' attention. The cuckoo chick is usually much larger than its foster parents and frequently exhausts them with its unending demands for food.

Rainbow Darter
Etheostoma caeruleum

Length: up to 3 inches
Diet: small crustaceans, insects, and snails
Method of Reproduction: egg layer

Home: United States and Canada
Order: Perchlike fishes
Family: Perches

 Fresh Water

 Fish

© GARY MESZAROS / PHOTO RESEARCHERS

Darters are among the smallest North American fish. Many of them, including the rainbow darter, are brilliantly colored, especially during breeding season. Rainbow darters are identified by the dark bars on their sides. The adult male's stripes are blue, alternating with red or orange stripes. The female has dark brown and pale yellow stripes. Young darters are brownish or olive-colored with especially broad, dark bars.

Like most darters, this species lives primarily at the bottom of streams or lakes. Typically it will rest quietly on the gravel until a disturbance prompts it to dart forward a few inches. These fish prefer fast, shallow water running over gravel and small stones. They are very common in the creeks and small rivers that drain into the Great Lakes and the Mississippi River.

Most rainbow darters spawn in late March. The male swims to a shallow area of rushing water. The female remains somewhat downstream in a pool of quieter water. When she is ready, she swims to her mate at the spawning area. He guards her excitedly, chasing away any competitors. Sometimes the male becomes so distracted by his rivals that the female returns downstream without spawning. When she does spawn, the female forces her head into the gravel and wriggles her body until the head is buried. The male settles on top of her, and they vibrate rapidly while mixing their eggs and sperm.

Roe Deer
Capreolus capreolus

Length of the Body: 3⅓ to 4½ feet
Length of the Tail: ½ to ¾ inch
Height at the Shoulder: 2 to 3 feet
Weight: 33 to 110 pounds

Diet: leaves, buds, grasses, fruits, and seeds
Number of Young: 1 to 4
Home: Eurasia
Order: Even-toed hoofed mammals
Family: Deer

 Forests and Mountains

 Mammals

© GEORGE MCCARTHY / CORBIS

In Europe, no wild animal is more common or familiar than the roe deer. Despite centuries of heavy hunting, roe deer still thrive. The species' natural habitat is the thick woods, where the deer live singly or in small families. But in places where farms have replaced forests, roe deer gather in large herds on open fields. Like North American deer, roe deer may become so numerous as to be pests. They are seldom a problem in spring or summer, however, when food is plentiful. But in winter, hungry deer often invade gardens and yards, and eat the tender parts of bushes and trees.

Most roe deer are born in May and June, weighing between 1 and 3 pounds. Twins are most common. Rather than follow their mother as she grazes, the newborn fawns lie concealed on the forest floor. Their white-spotted coat is good camouflage. But should a predator attack the fawn, the young deer will call for help with a piercing cry. The mother then charges to the rescue.

Young roe deer bucks grow their first set of antlers before they are a year old. They shed their antlers annually, usually right after mating season in the fall. A new set of horns sprouts each spring. At first the antlers are covered with a thick, velvety skin. The buck scrapes off this protective coating by rubbing its horns against trees and rocks. The torn skin can look gruesome as it hangs in bloody tatters from the buck's antlers. But it does not hurt the animal.

Bush Dog
Speothos venaticus

Length of the Body: 2 to 2½ feet
Length of the Tail: 4½ to 6 inches
Diet: rodents, deer, and other animals

Weight: 11 to 15 pounds
Number of Young: 4 to 6
Home: South America
Order: Carnivores
Family: Dogs

 Rain forests

 Mammals

© MARTIN B. WITHERS / FRANK LANE PICTURE AGENCY / CORBIS

The bush dog looks much like a little bear, with a round, muscular body, small ears, and squat legs. It also has a short, bearlike tail, the smallest of any wild dog. The bush dog's unusual compact shape helps it move easily through tangled bushes and vines. It is at home both in rain forests and dry woodlands, as well as treeless grasslands.

The bush dog may look cute and cuddly, and many have been tamed. But in the wild, it is an aggressive hunter that will attack animals many times its size. Bush dogs frequently kill armadillos and then take over their prey's den. Sometimes bush dogs hunt in family packs of four to six dogs. Biologists have even seen two packs joined together in a hunt. One group hides in ambush while the second group chases deer or other prey into the waiting trap.

Because the bush dog has always been rare, scientists know little about its family life. Before she gives birth, a pregnant female probably digs a den with the help of her mate. From bush dogs in captivity, we know that the father actively helps with childbirth. He licks the newborn bush dog pups clean as they emerge from their mother's womb, and then he bites off their umbilical cords. When the pups are a little older, the father brings back food from his stomach. By bumping their snouts against his, the young beg him to regurgitate the meal.

41

Spinner Dolphin
Stenella longirostris

Length of the Body: about 6 feet
Weight: about 165 pounds
Diet: fish and squid
Number of Young: 1

Home: all tropical oceans
Order: Whales, dolphins, and porpoises
Family: Dolphins

 Oceans and Shores

 Mammals

© KEVIN SCHAFER / CORBIS

Spinner dolphins joyfully spin through the air as they leap out of the water. A spinner can rotate as many as seven times in a single leap. Marine biologists believe that these gymnasts of the seas spin and leap simply for the fun of it. For the same reason, they love to chase ships, jumping in the waves made by the bow. Spinner dolphins are distinguished from similar dolphin species by their long snout. Their species name, *longirostris*, literally means "longbeak."

Unfortunately, many spinners are killed each year by tuna fishermen. The dolphins often swim above large schools of tuna. The appearance of the dolphins is a signal to the fishermen that tuna are near, so the fishermen set their traps beneath the dolphins. When the fishermen reel in their nets, dolphins are caught along with the valuable tuna. As a result, many dolphins are accidentally killed. Today tuna fishermen must make a special effort to free the dolphins from their nets. The spinner dolphin's only natural enemies are large, predatory sharks.

These dolphins often gather in schools of more than 1,000 members. In summer and autumn, they mate. The female gives birth to a 3- to 4-foot-long baby nearly a year later. Dolphins mature in about 3 years and can live as long as 30 years.

Fat Dormouse
Glis glis

Length: 5 to 8 inches
Weight: 2½ to 6 ounces
Diet: fruit, nuts, seeds, insects, eggs

Number of Young: 3 to 7
Home: Europe
Order: Rodents
Family: Dormice

 Forests and Mountains

Mammals

© ERNIE JAMES / NHPA

The leaves of a large oak rustle at nightfall, acorns roll on the ground, and suddenly a long bushy tail disappears into a thicket. Is it a squirrel? No, it's a dormouse, a little rodent just as swift and fond of nuts as a squirrel.

Every night a fat dormouse searches trees for seeds, acorns, berries, and other fruits. Once in a while, it creates chaos in orchards and in vineyards, eating ripe as well as green fruits. It also eats insects. In fact, it eats all it can to produce reserves of fat for the winter. And that is why it is called the "fat" dormouse. In September or October, the dormouse falls into a deep sleep, rolled up in a hollow tree trunk, a stump, or a hole dug in the ground. It will not wake up until April or May, which is why we sometimes use the expression "to sleep like a dormouse." But the sleepy dormouse in *Alice in Wonderland* was probably not a fat dormouse. It must have been an even sleepier relative, the common dormouse, *Muscardinus avellanarius*, which sleeps all day in the summer as well as all the time in the winter.

In June or July the mating season begins. In August or September, three to seven young come into the world. Their mother stays close to them and cares for them on her own for a few days. The female welcomes the male into the nest around the 16th day. The father is very helpful: he cleans and helps protect his young. The family stays together until the following spring.

Garden Dormouse
Eliomys quercinus

Length of the Body: 4 to 6 inches
Length of the Tail: 4 to 5 inches
Diet: small animals, seeds, fruits, and leaves

Weight: 2 to 6 ounces
Number of Young: 4 to 6
Home: continental Europe, North Africa, and the Sinai
Order: Rodents
Family: Dormicelike rodents

 Forests and Mountains

 Mammals

© SUZANNE DANEGGER / JACANA / PHOTO RESEARCHERS

Dormice get their name from the French word *dormire*, meaning "to sleep," because they hibernate through much of the winter. As you might have guessed from its full name, the garden dormouse likes to live around humans. It will even sneak in from the garden to snoop through the family kitchen. However, this nocturnal (active at night) creature is more of a pest killer than a pest. Like all dormice, the garden species eats fruits and seeds. But it prefers to gobble down such common pests as house mice, spiders, and snails.

The garden dormouse builds its nest among stones on the ground or in a tree hole. It lines its cubbyhole with leaves, twigs, feathers, and bits of fur and cow hair.

At sunset the dormouse wakens from its slumber, blinks its large black eyes—and scurries into the night.

While other species of dormice have thick, bushy tails, the tail of the garden dormouse is almost hairless, except for a white tuft of thick fur at the end. Garden dormice are born with tails almost as long as their bodies. Strangely enough, many adult garden dormice have much shorter tails. To understand why, just try to grab a garden dormouse from behind. Its tail skin will come right off in your hand. When the wound dries, the dormouse just bites off the shriveled end. The tail will not regrow in length, but the tip will sprout a new bushy tassel.